Let's Have a Cuppa

Life's Brew of Stories and Wisdom, Poured for Comfort and Peace

by Smile Trinidad

Let's Have a Cuppa
Copyright © 2026 by Smile Trinidad

All rights reserved. This book or any portion thereof may not be reproduced, distributed, or transmitted in any form or by any means, including photocopying, recording, or other electronic or mechanical methods, without the prior written permission of the publisher, except in the case of brief quotations embodied in critical reviews and certain other noncommercial uses permitted by copyright law.

Published by The Fil-Am Cam

ISBN (Hardcover): 979-8-9933606-0-7

For permission requests, write to the author at the contact below:

The Fil-Am Cam
TheFilAmCam@gmail.com

To my husband, Jose, for the unconditional love
that holds me even when I feel unlovable.

To my daughter, EMa, whose spirit inspires me
to never stop learning and growing.

And to my family and friends, who have
filled my life with laughter and grace.

Your presence is the most beautiful brew of all.

Welcome. Please pull up a chair and let's find a quiet moment together and have a cuppa.

This little book is a journal of lessons from my own journey, a sweet brew of stories and wisdom steeped in the simple moments of my life.

These pages are an invitation to slow down, settle in with your favourite cup of tea and have a little chat with yourself or a friend. My fondest hope is that in these stories, you discover a reflection of your own beautiful path.

This book is also a testament to the life that has shaped me ~ a life spent lovingly healing my pains and joyfully celebrating my wins. I'm always growing, always learning, always sharing every blessing. To God be all the glory.

Now take a sip and let's begin.

~ Sm!Le ♡

CONTENTS

Part 1: The Inner Journey

Part 2: The Path to Connection

Part 3: Embracing Abundance
and Finding Peace

"I can do all things through Him who strengthens me."
Philippians 4:13

What is success to me?

To see and appreciate the quiet miracles of everyday life;
To love and accept myself in my brokenness,
and to find healing from the sorrows I've experienced;
To find and keep even a single true friend;
To love and feel loved;
To be someone's source of strength and inspiration;
To be able to rest at night with a peaceful heart;
To help lead even one person back to their faith in God;
To know in my heart that I gave my best,
so I can leave this life with no regrets.
This, to me, is to have succeeded.

What is success to you?

"I praise You, for I am fearfully and wonderfully made.
Wonderful are Your works; my soul knows it very well."
Psalm 139:14

The Inner Journey

The most meaningful path we will ever take is the one that leads us home to ourselves.

We all yearn to be loved and accepted for who we are,
yet hide our true selves in fear of judgment.
We forget that

*vulnerability is but
a quiet courage*

to open our hearts and find the
deep, genuine connections we seek.

When we reconnected after more than a decade, Jose and I were two lives on opposite sides of the world, yet our conversations flowed without effort. He was in California and I was in Manila, and with both of us having no interest in a long-distance relationship, our friendship was a rare gift. We were free to be entirely ourselves, unburdened by the need to impress or to please.

Over the months, our conversations moved from casual chats about work to a deeper exchange of fears and dreams. I found myself so completely seen and accepted around him, that a quiet shift happened. We weren't looking for a romance ~ we were just two friends who naturally, and inevitably, fell in love.

This experience taught me to be braver in letting my true self be seen. I've learned to accept that while people will always have their opinions, the ones who are truly meant for my life will appreciate me for exactly who I am.

What is the quiet truth you are holding back,
and what connection might be waiting
on the other side?

The most rewarding journey
you can take is the

journey back to yourself

As you get to know who you truly are,
the opinions of others will matter
less and less.

This is a lesson I've learned from a Filipino word I've heard my whole life: "maarte." It's used to describe someone who is picky, dramatic, or finicky. I was called maarte because I like dressing up, I don't eat dinuguan (pork blood), I easily cry, I love pink, and I scream when I see a cockroach.

I used to take offense but now, when someone calls me maarte, I say "thank you!"

I say thank you because I have learned to understand that part of myself. I know now that I cry easily because I'm in touch with my emotions. (I laugh easily too!) I have preferences because I know what I like and enjoy. And just like everyone else, I have my own tastes, fears, and quirks.

I also know that I'm compassionate, artistic, helpful, friendly, and funny, among other things. Maarte is just a part of who I truly am.

So, if people told me my green hair was ugly, it would mean nothing to me because I know my hair is black. I know who I am, and how people define me will not change how I see myself.

What is one belief you hold about yourself
that is stronger than any opinion you've ever heard?

Forgiveness is about releasing the pain that binds you to a person or experience. It is *a gift of freedom and peace* that you give yourself.

As the fairytale-loving, idealistic young lady that I was, I once fell for sweet words and promises. I entered a relationship that was beautiful on the surface, yet was filled with a quiet emotional and, at times, physical pain. Over and over, he would walk away, but believing that loving someone meant accepting them unconditionally, I would always welcome him back.

It took me years to understand that what I was in was not love, and I was finally ready to leave the cycle behind. One ordinary night, without a fight, I handed him a letter to thank him for the happy moments and to wish him well. I did not hate him and, in my heart, I had already forgiven him even without his apology.

For a long time, I carried the feeling that I had wasted my youth on a love that repeatedly hurt me. But eventually, I found peace in the lessons I learned and, most importantly, I forgave myself for the decisions I made with a heart that was just trying to love. I now remember those years free from pain, and with much love for my younger self whose strength led me to where I am today.

What memory or hurt
are you ready to gently set down
to accept the gift of freedom and
peace for yourself?

I love to host. To see the people I care for gathered, their laughter echoing in our home, fills my heart with joy. I pour myself into every detail, from planning the menu and baking ahead to making sure our guests are as comfortable as can be.

But as much as I love giving, it can also be draining. So at times, when I know everyone is content, I would quietly slip into our bedroom to find a moment of rest. It always makes me smile to find Jose there too, my happy companion in the art of slowing down. A few moments away from the crowd is all it takes to simply breathe and be ready once more to be a gracious hostess.

Sometimes, life can be exhausting. I've learned that while a grand vacation may not always be possible, true rest can be found in the small, everyday moments. A few minutes sipping my favourite tea, a quiet moment in a cozy corner with a book, or simply savouring a fifteen-minute bath is all it takes. To be fully immersed in a moment of peace, no matter how brief, is enough for me to feel recharged and ready to give my best to the world again.

What small, daily ritual of care
will you prioritize to replenish your heart
and give from a place of abundance?

I've come to think of our minds as gardens.
We get to choose the seeds we plant,
and we have to be aware of the weeds that take root.

Cultivating a beautiful mind takes care and attention

When we were still living in Singapore, I began to spend my free time watching videos of luxury bags on social media. I found myself focusing on the things I could buy to look nice and fit in. It was a tempting and endless cycle of consuming and desiring.

After a while, I grew tired of the chase. I decided to put that same energy towards my inner world, and began to fill my free time with books and videos that inspire me to focus on my values and growth.

I truly became what I consumed. When I read about self-improvement, I found myself striving to improve. And when I constantly read the Bible, I grew closer to God.

While I still appreciate all the beautiful things, my self-confidence no longer comes from society's approval. Instead, it comes from the deeper well of knowing that I have the power to choose what fills my mind, and that choice has the power to change my life. With that, I am a work in progress, firm in my values and committed to becoming a better version of myself.

What is one thought
you will consciously choose to nurture,
knowing that it will bring more beauty
and peace to your inner garden?

"Be completely humble and gentle;
be patient, bearing with one another in love."
Ephesians 4:2

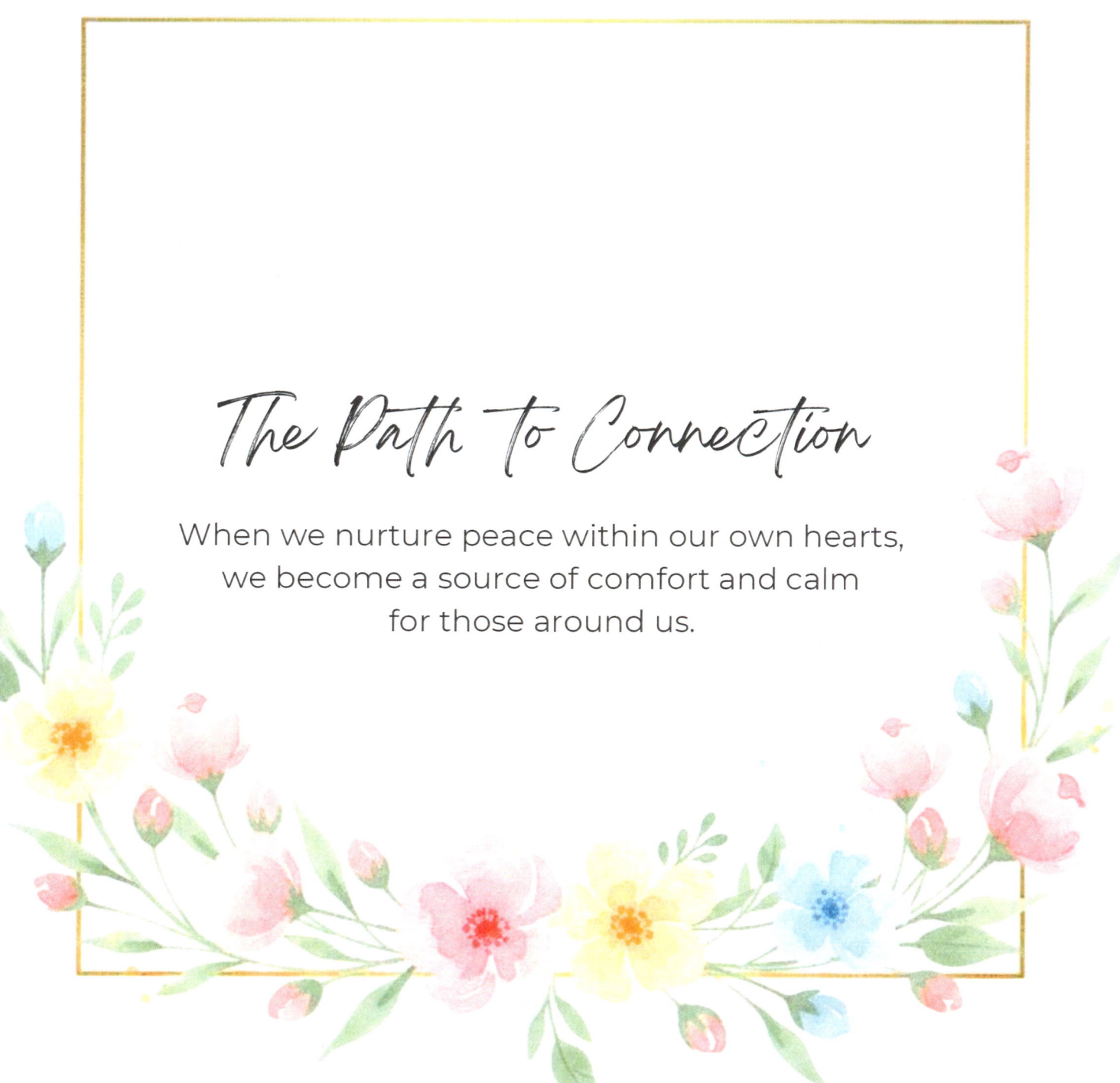

The Path to Connection

When we nurture peace within our own hearts,
we become a source of comfort and calm
for those around us.

I've learned that most arguments
are not really about what they seem.
In the quiet heart of most conflicts lies

the three fundamental human desires

To have a secure and gentle connection.
To be valued, respected, and recognized.
To be heard and to have an equal voice.

My first real argument with my husband, Jose, wasn't about a big betrayal or a major life decision. It was over a pile of dirty dishes, and it's not what you'd expect it to be.

That might sound silly, but it hit me hard. I'd gone to the kitchen, ready to do the dishes as I always did, only to find the sink empty and sparkling. Jose, looking proud, explained he'd already taken care of them to be helpful. Instead of feeling grateful, a wave of anger washed over me, so strong it surprised us both. He couldn't understand why his simple act of kindness made me so upset.

Of course, the dishes weren't the real problem. After a decade-long career, I had moved to Singapore to be with him, leaving my professional life behind. My new role felt centered on the household, and his simple act of taking over a chore felt like a quiet removal of my purpose. It made me feel unneeded, a little bit useless. He, in turn, was just trying to show his love and support, and my reaction deeply confused and hurt him.

In the end, we realized that while he was simply fighting to be valued and respected, what I was truly longing for was a shared sense of purpose and a recognized ability to contribute. By digging deep, we understood each other better, and that small fight over a clean sink became a turning point that helped us grow, not just as a couple, but as individuals, too.

What unmet desire, masked by a recent conflict, is asking for your attention?

Let us not be quick to judge, because
we do not know everyone's whole story.
Instead, let us
*be quick to show compassion
and give grace*
because everyone is carrying
a burden we cannot see.

When I was in fifth grade, our class had an activity where we were assigned to groups. I was badly bullied, so when my name was called and assigned with the bullies, I quietly muttered a complaint to myself as I walked to the group. A moderator overheard me, and the activity came to a sudden halt. For the next 20 minutes, I was the sole focus of my class advisor's lecture. She stood before the whole class, looked me in the eyes, and with a pointed finger, insisted that I apologize.

I was just a child, yet not one adult ~ not among the teachers or nuns ~ bothered to ask me why I felt the way I did. It was a moment of deep loneliness, a feeling that no one cared or understood. And because of that, I want to be the kind of person who asks, listens, and understands so no one else has to feel the way I did.

I know that there is so much more to every person than the little I can see. Maybe their spouse is sick, they lost their job, or they buried a parent yesterday. These are not written on their faces, and I will never know everyone's story.

Because of this, I strive to remember that every person deserves my compassion and grace, whether I know their whole story or not.

What invisible burden do you carry,
and how does remembering that burden
inspire you to show compassion to others?

Some hearts are teapots
built to hold and pour from a place of great abundance,
while others are teacups
meant to be gently filled and sipped.
The secret to a genuine understanding is to honour the grace
of our own capacity and the measure of another's heart.

My sister and I are extremely close. We share the same core values and enjoy many of the same things, but we handle situations with very different hearts. I am a natural feeler who focuses on grand plans, while she is a practical thinker who favours simplicity.

This difference became clear one day during my visit to see our family. I, the teapot, wanted our gathering to include out-of-town trips, planned activities, and coordinating outfits for that perfect family photo. As the one who lives far from home, my heart clings to every rare opportunity to make each moment with them extra special. Meanwhile, my sister, the teacup, who seldom gets a chance to unwind, was happy with casual family gatherings at home and simply wanted to savour our moments together, unburdened by a grand plan.

In the end, we realized a simple truth: I was looking for a special memory to hold on to, while she was simply looking for a peaceful moment. In that quiet understanding, we learned to make room for each other. And the beautiful picture we created that day became a quiet testament to the love that exists, not in spite of our differences, but because of them.

Are you a teapot or a teacup?
Knowing your own capacity,
how can you best honour
the measure of another's heart?

The greatest rewards in life
are found not by waiting
but by the persistent courage to
create them for yourself

I moved from the Philippines to Singapore to be with my husband, Jose. I didn't know anyone there, and a new place without a single friend felt very lonely.

I tried to meet people through different groups, but there was no click, no spark of connection. Instead of giving up, I decided to build my own community, and created an online group for stay-at-home wives like me.

The beginning was slow. It was just one friend at first, then two, but soon enough our group grew. Our gatherings evolved from simple meet-ups into playdates with the kids and dinners with our husbands. We became a chosen family, celebrating every special occasion together, from birthdays to Christmases.

Now, years later, many of us have moved back to our different countries, but we continue to keep in touch. I'm grateful for the persistence that led me to find more than just friends ~ it led me to find my Singapore family.

What is the first courageous step you can take today to create the reward you know you deserve?

In any difficult moment, look for the
people with kind hearts
Their actions are a quiet testament
that goodness is always present in the world.

I was at a mall in Manila one time, waiting to meet a friend, when I was suddenly struck with a severe pain in my abdomen. I remember praying, "Lord, if it's Your will for me to die now, I will happily accept my fate. But please don't let me die alone, without anyone I know."

Being visibly in pain, a stranger offered to help me. I gave him my mobile phone and money to make a call. I knew he could easily take everything and leave, but he did not. He even went beyond that and got medical help for me.

Just a few hours after my first ambulance ride, I had a major operation to save me from what could have been a fatal medical situation. I wasn't able to ask for the person's name, and I can't even remember his face because I was curled up in pain. But to this day, I pray that he is living a good life.

It's difficult to trust just anyone, so I strive to be that person who can help and be trusted. I look for ways to help, even in my own little ways. When I see a family trying to take a photo together, I offer to take it for them. When someone is sick, I bring them a home-cooked meal. When a friend is troubled, I listen and offer prayers and encouragement.

The news is filled with stories that make us believe there's so much evil in the world. While there will always be challenging situations, kind people will also always be there. And if, in that rare occasion we can't find one, remember that we have the power to be one.

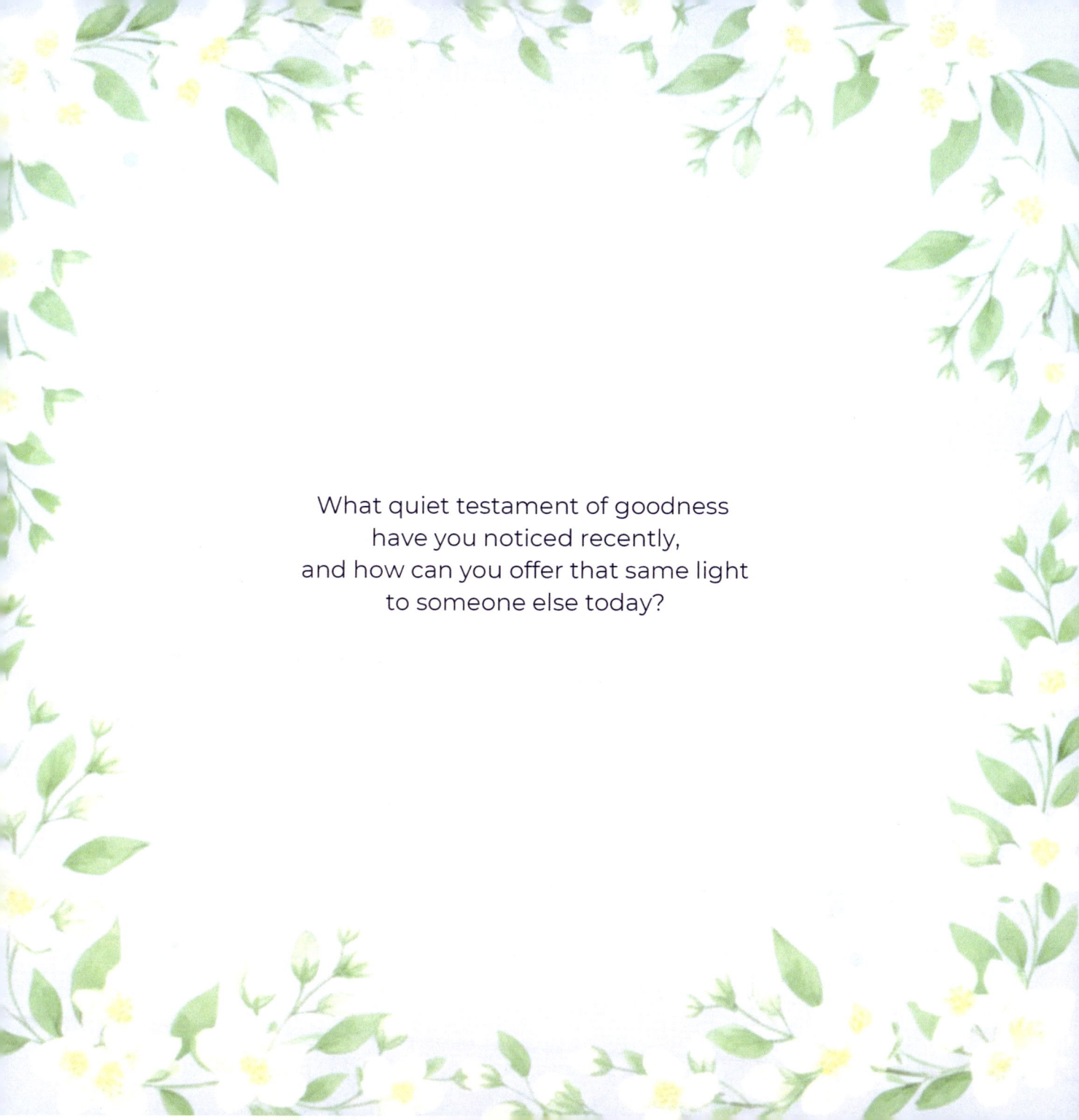

What quiet testament of goodness
have you noticed recently,
and how can you offer that same light
to someone else today?

"Trust in the Lord with all your heart,
and do not lean on your own understanding."
Proverbs 3:5

Embracing Abundance and Finding Peace

The profound peace we pursue comes from realizing that all the meaning and joy we seek already resides within us.

A grateful heart makes a peaceful life

It is the lens through which we learn to see the miraculous in the mundane.

When I was younger, our summer vacations took us to my father's province in Pagudpud, Ilocos Norte. I loved the amazing beaches, but I remember a gentle shock in realizing that the big, old, wooden house he grew up in ~ with its large, beautiful capiz windows ~ had a bathroom a few feet outside, and the water had to be manually lifted from a well. As a child, it was both a humbling and hilarious experience to take a bath within a wall of coconut leaves, feeling the open air above. I loved those summer vacations, but I always returned home with appreciation for the simple luxury of an indoor bathroom.

As I grew older, I realized I had to intentionally cultivate a grateful heart. By simply naming three things I was thankful for every night, it became clear how many countless blessings I receive daily, and how many I had once taken for granted.

This new perspective changed my entire outlook. After a long day of walking, I now find myself thankful for my strong legs rather than complaining. When stuck in traffic, I appreciate the simple fact that we have a car instead of getting frustrated. And when I feel the pressure to cook and keep our house clean, I find joy in being able to do it for my family and home that I love. Gratefulness has become a way of life, giving me greater peace and happiness as I've learned to appreciate the beautiful reality of all the simple gifts in my life.

What ordinary moment today,
seen through the lens of gratitude,
revealed a quiet miracle?

The most special moments are the ones we're in

Don't save your beautiful things for a "special" day ~ use them to make today a little more beautiful.

In my childhood home, we didn't have anything expensive. I never even had a Barbie doll of my own. But I remember in my friend's home, her pristine Barbie dolls were sealed in their boxes, gleaming on display. I always saw it as a kind of silent tragedy ~ a waste of fun tucked away collecting dust.

When I was finally able to own beautiful things, I realized their value isn't just in their price, but in the joy they bring me. I have a simple rule I call my "cost per use math". For example, if I have a $3,000 purse and only used it on 10 special occasions a year, each time would have a high cost of $300. But if I use it almost every day ~ say 300 times a year ~ the cost per use drops to just $10! That way, I get the most out of what I paid for and, more importantly, I get to feel the joy of using a beautiful item every single day.

Some people use their best china when they have guests, or wear their pretty dresses for significant events. But for me, using my treasured items is an act of self-kindness. When I use a beautiful purse, a delicate teacup, or a pretty dress for a quiet moment, it's like telling myself that I am worthy of this joy. And every day I am alive is a special occasion that I intend to celebrate.

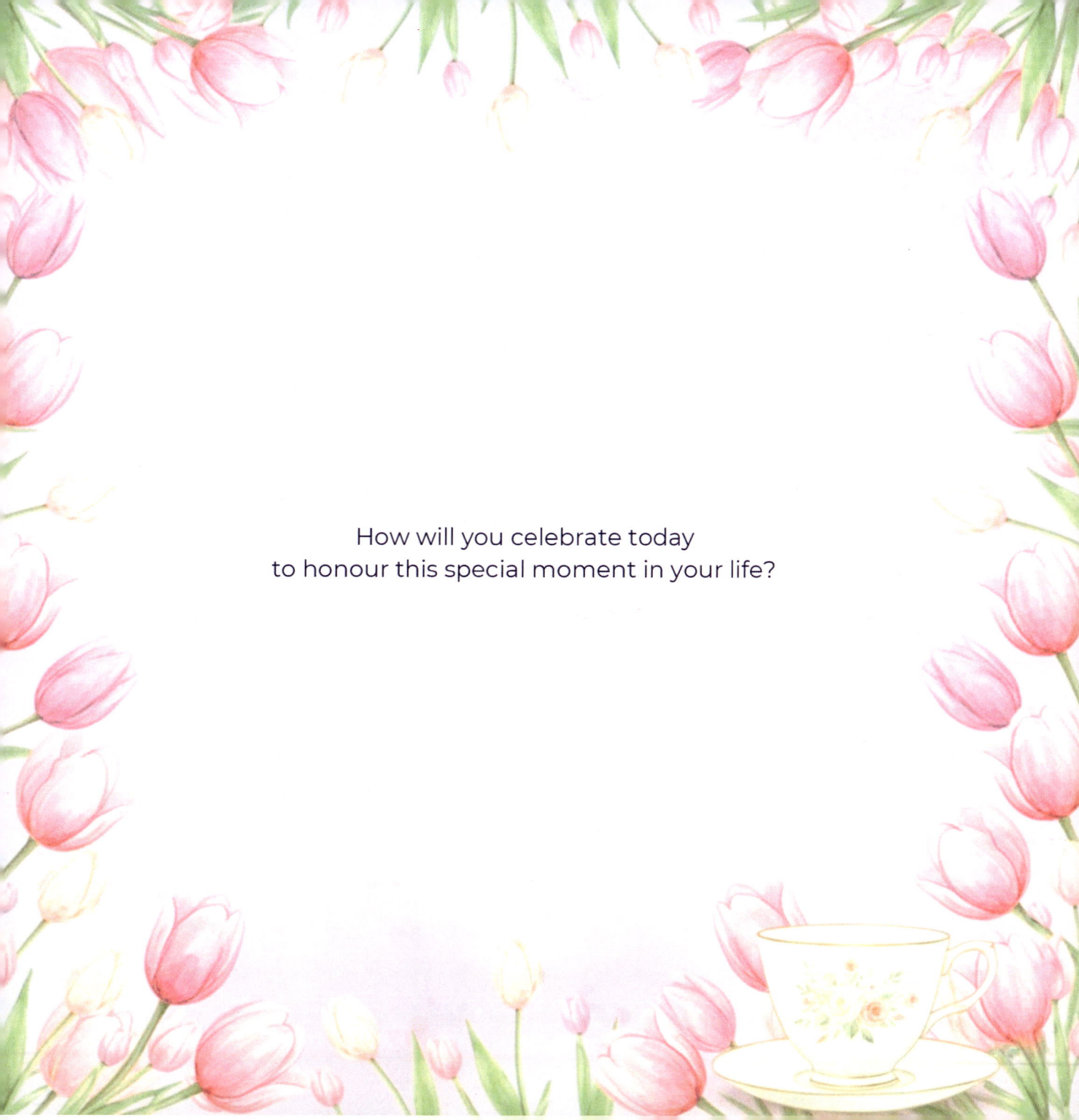

How will you celebrate today
to honour this special moment in your life?

A life rich in memories is a life well-lived

Our deepest happiness comes from the beautiful collection of moments we create with the people we love.

I have always loved to travel. The excitement of visiting a new place, trying unfamiliar food, and meeting people from different cultures has always filled me with joy. I am so blessed to have a husband who shares this love for exploring the world.

When we bought our house, it needed a lot of work. To save money for our adventures, I took on the job of painting the interior myself. It was a long, laborious process, but the money we saved became our reward: a trip to New York. We were both amazed by the beauty of Niagara Falls and made wonderful memories together.

I can no longer remember the name of the paint color I used for the walls, but I can still vividly recall laughing with my husband as the water from the falls sprinkled our faces, and him running to catch my handkerchief as the wind blew it away. Now, that moment is just one of many memories captured in a photo, hanging on the very walls I painted. And while we may leave our house one day, the memories will stay in the home of our hearts forever.

What beautiful moment
would you like to create
to add joy and peace that
will be treasured in your heart?

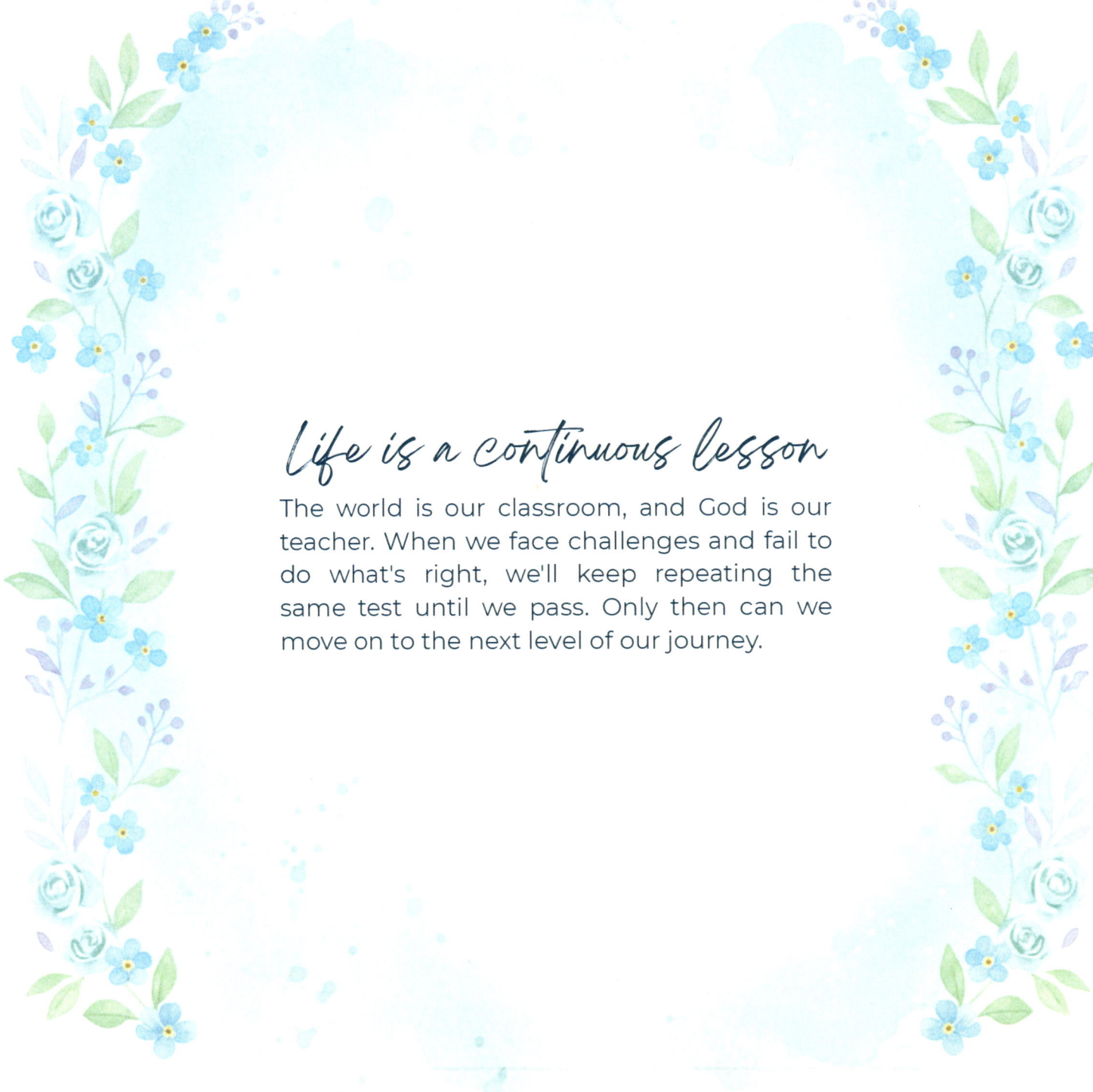

Life is a continuous lesson

The world is our classroom, and God is our teacher. When we face challenges and fail to do what's right, we'll keep repeating the same test until we pass. Only then can we move on to the next level of our journey.

Self-worth was a hard lesson for me to learn. I was bullied when I was a child, from elementary until high school. My classmates' words were meant to make me feel bad about myself, and they succeeded. I truly believed I wasn't enough ~ not smart enough, not pretty enough, not talented enough. That feeling followed me year after year.

While I struggled in school, I leaned into art as a therapy. In my senior year, I took a chance and applied for our school's prestigious art class. I gained confidence in my abilities when I got accepted, and it slowly changed how I saw myself. By the time I entered college, I had a new sense of self-assurance that helped me thrive in class and build a healthier social life.

When I realized that I am enough ~ enough to be treated nicely, to deserve good friends, and to be accepted as the imperfect me ~ my struggle ended. As I learned my own value and self-worth, I didn't just grow; I blossomed.

What lesson is the universe offering you right now, and what small wisdom will you claim to pass the test?

Trust in God's plan

The purpose of our paths
may be hidden from us now,
but in time, the fragments will reveal
a beautiful and purposeful whole.
Rest in this truth, for He is always with us.

School was not my strength. When I didn't get into the university where my brother and sister went, I was devastated. But I ended up loving my university where I built my confidence and met lifetime friends.

For our final year, our class was assigned to different companies for on-the-job training. I liked the company I was assigned to and hoped they would hire me after I graduated. Unfortunately, my classmate and I were treated poorly. So instead of finishing our training with them, we found another place to work and ended up at the company where our friends were. I loved it! ~ the people, the place, and the job! I was even hired before graduation!

It was an airline company and I was able to travel a lot, thanks to our flight benefits. During one of my trips, I reconnected with a high school acquaintance who ended up becoming my wonderful husband!

Looking back, as much as it was hard to go through the disappointments, I can clearly see how all those events had to happen to lead me to where I am now. I know I am exactly where I am meant to be, and I believe it will all end well. If I'm not in a good place, then I know it's not yet the end. I just need to keep trusting and keep going.

Looking back, what uncertain path turned out to be a quiet redirection that aligned you perfectly with God's plan?

"Oh give thanks to the Lord, for He is good,
for His steadfast love endures forever!"
Psalm 107:1

Thank you for accepting my invitation to have a cuppa. Your time is a precious gift, and I'm truly grateful you chose to spend these quiet moments sharing a cup with me through these pages.

My hope is that this book has brought you a sense of peace and a gentle reminder of the beautiful, imperfect path you are on. May your own journey through life be filled with hope, joy, and the blessing of God.

~ Sm!Le ♡

www.ingramcontent.com/pod-product-compliance
Lightning Source LLC
Chambersburg PA
CBRC091934130526
44582CB00049B/183